Working in Harmony

Lesley Halferty
Art by Simone Krüger

Literacy Consultants
David Booth • Kathleen Corrigan

Contents

Chapter 1
An Unhappy Pair 4

Chapter 2
Unequal Partners 8

Chapter 3
A Miserable Day 12

Chapter 4
Music and Lights 16

Chapter 5
A Strange and Lonely Place 24

Chapter 6
A Great Day 28

Chapter 1

An Unhappy Pair

Emma was excited and a little nervous. Today was the day the class would be broken into pairs for the class's final project. Emma would have to spend a lot of time working with her partner during and even after school.

Of course, Emma hoped her partner would be her best friend, Zoe. Emma and Zoe had been friends since kindergarten, and they saw each other after school and on weekends all the time, so working together would be a breeze. Also, any excuse to spend more time talking to Zoe made Emma happy.

As Mr. Grady called out the names of the pairs, Emma and Zoe exchanged excited glances. Surely he would put them together because he and everyone else at school knew that they were best friends. But when Mr. Grady called Zoe's name, he paired her with Liz instead. Zoe seemed OK with it, because she and Liz got along pretty well, but Emma's heart sank.

When Mr. Grady called her name, Emma sat up straight and held her breath. She crossed her fingers and hoped for a partner with whom she'd get along.

"Emma's partner will be Arjun," announced Mr. Grady. Emma deflated.

Arjun was a boy who had recently moved to the neighborhood from India. He was very quiet. He never participated in class and did not say much to the other kids. At recess and lunch, he kept to himself and never played with anyone. In fact, Emma couldn't even recall seeing him smile. She certainly did not know anything about him and had never seen him outside of school. Emma had a sinking feeling this partnership would not go well. She tried to be positive and thought, "Maybe he won't be so shy when it's just the two of us talking."

She had no such luck.

After Mr. Grady finished assigning the pairs, he asked the partners to sit together and have a little chat in order to start planning for their project. All throughout their meeting, Arjun sat in complete silence while Emma brainstormed ideas. The assignment was to present a family tradition to the class and explain its meaning and origin.

Emma suggested the tradition of eating turkey at Thanksgiving dinner. Arjun didn't seem particularly excited by the idea. Emma wanted Arjun to feel comfortable and involved with the project, so she then suggested the tradition of decorating the tree at Christmas. Aside from opening presents, decorating the tree was Emma's favorite part of Christmas. She couldn't imagine anyone disliking this tradition. To her disappointment, Arjun merely nodded in response, and he continued to stare at the table without speaking.

Chapter 2

Unequal Partners

When Emma got home, she went straight to her room and slumped over her bed. She was frustrated with Arjun and more than a little hurt because he had just sat there the whole time letting her do all the work. He never once offered to help. He hardly even looked at her!

Emma's mother came into the room and sat down beside her. "Do you want to talk about it?" she asked, letting Emma take the lead. Emma sat up and told her mom everything, about not being paired with Zoe and about the horrible, one-sided chat she'd had with Arjun. Her frustration was building, and just the thought of his silence made her even more upset and sad.

"I just don't know why he wouldn't talk to me," Emma said. "It's as if he'd already decided he didn't want to be my friend before knowing anything about me."

Emma's mom rubbed her back and said quietly, "I know how hard you work on your school projects, Emma. I also know how much you like making friends." Emma sniffed and nodded. "But maybe sometimes you're too hard on yourself, and maybe sometimes you're too hard on other people too." Her mom smiled gently. Emma looked down at her lap.

Emma's mom reminded her that Arjun had only moved here from India last school year. She added, "Can you imagine how much he must be missing his life back in India?"

Emma promised her mom that she would try to be more understanding of Arjun's feelings, but secretly she was still upset. How bad could it be? What could he be missing so much that he would be so rude to her?

The next morning, the knot in Emma's chest was still there. She headed to school in a funk, and when she got there, she avoided Arjun until it was time for their meeting. Even then, she just sat in her chair and crossed her arms. "Let him do some work," Emma thought.

They passed the whole of their time together in silence. Mr. Grady watched them from the front of the room with a thoughtful look on his face. But he didn't interfere. Emma would glance toward Arjun from time to time, but if she saw him looking at her, she'd huff and look away. When their time was up, Emma was the first to get up and leave the classroom.

Emma went straight to the girls' bathroom and shut herself up in a stall. She'd been trying to make Arjun do his share of the work, but she'd only succeeded in making herself feel bad. The worst part was they were no closer to starting their project. Emma went home even more frustrated and sad than she'd been the day before.

Chapter 3

A Miserable Day

The next day, Emma did not want to go to school. She did not want to tell her mom what was bothering her either. She knew that her mom would be disappointed at how childish she had been the day before and would tell her to apologize to Arjun. But the thought of that just made Emma even angrier. Why should she apologize? She hadn't started it. To avoid her mom's questions, Emma got out of bed and dragged herself to school.

When she got to class, Emma noticed right away that Arjun wasn't there. She wondered where he was and if maybe he was sick. But she quickly remembered she was upset with him. She was glad she didn't have to see him today. Emma spent her meeting time making a list of ornaments her family usually hung on their Christmas tree.

At recess Zoe and Emma sat down on the grass together. Emma wanted to tell Zoe all about her troubles with Arjun, but Zoe only wanted to tell Emma how well things were going with Liz. Emma listened and tried to be happy for her friend, but just as she started to confide to Zoe about her bad luck, Liz joined them.

Sitting down between them, Liz started talking as if the three of them had been best friends forever. Zoe didn't seem to mind; in fact, she seemed quite happy that Liz was there. Irritated at Liz's presence, Emma got grouchier and couldn't muster a laugh when Liz told a joke.

When Liz ran off to talk to someone, Zoe took the opportunity to say, "That was rude, Emma."

Emma didn't know how to respond. "What are you talking about?" she managed to ask.

"The way you were with Liz," Zoe replied. "You totally ignored her."

"No, I didn't!" Emma was so flustered that she couldn't explain herself properly. A flush spread across her cheeks and her eyes flashed. "Why are you mad at me? Just because I didn't laugh at a joke your new best friend made? It wasn't funny anyway!" she said loudly.

It was not what she had meant to say, but the words had rushed out of her before she'd had time to think about them. Zoe's expression hardened. She didn't say anything to Emma and simply stomped away.

Now things were really falling apart. Emma thought about how happy and excited she'd been only two days ago, and now she felt miserable. It was all Arjun's fault. She had never been so mad at anyone before as she was now at Arjun. She thought about asking Mr. Grady to give her a new partner, but she was too proud. Emma flopped down onto the grass and wrote off yet another miserable day.

Chapter 4

Music and Lights

In the afternoon the whole class headed down the hall to the music room. For the last three weeks, Ms. Aguilar, their music teacher, had been taking them through a unit called "Celebration Through Music." She had been teaching them about celebrations in different cultures by playing music from around the world. The music she played and the stories she told always sounded so fascinating.

The class moved toward the music room in anticipation. Ms. Aguilar had yet to disappoint.

Music was drifting from the music room down the hall toward them. It reminded Emma of a Bollywood movie she had once seen. There was a main female vocal supported by a background chorus. The lyrics were in a language Emma didn't recognize.

The students all gasped when they entered the room. Once Emma's eyes adjusted to the light, she looked around in wonder.

The whole music room had been decorated with brightly colored scarves. There were strings of lights and multicolored paper lanterns hanging from wall to wall. On a table in the center of the room, there was a large, shallow bowl filled with water. Floating on the surface of the water were beautiful flowers, and around the bowl were several LED candles in clay holders. Ms. Aguilar had turned off the fluorescent ceiling lights so that the candles and lanterns cast a warm glow about the room.

Ms. Aguilar asked the class if anyone knew what celebration they were discussing today. Nobody answered. "Maybe Arjun can tell us." Ms. Aguilar looked around.

"Arjun isn't here today," someone offered.

Ms. Aguilar looked disappointed. "That's too bad!" she exclaimed. "He would have been able to tell us from a much more personal perspective. But no matter. Today we are talking about Diwali. Can anyone guess in which country this festival is celebrated?"

Emma could guess. If Arjun knew about it, and Arjun was from India, then the answer was obvious.

"In India?" she asked aloud.

"That's right! Very good, Emma!" Ms. Aguilar looked impressed. Normally, Emma would have been overjoyed about the praise, but right now she was feeling very guilty for some reason.

Ms. Aguilar went on to explain Diwali. It was celebrated in October or November of every year. In fact, Ms. Aguilar explained, it was being celebrated this very week in India and by Hindus all over the world.

"Is Arjun Hindu?" Emma wondered to herself. She also wondered what being Hindu meant.

Ms. Aguilar continued to explain that Diwali began as a harvest festival, and its purpose was to celebrate the last harvest before winter. It was the largest festival celebrated in India, marked by family gatherings, fireworks, bonfires, sharing of sweets, and the worship of Lakshmi, the goddess of wealth.

"That sounds a lot like Christmas," said a classmate.

"There are certainly several similarities," said Ms. Aguilar. "And just like Christmas, an important part of the celebration is the music people play. The song you heard as you walked in is called 'Om Jai Lakshmi Mata.' It is a Hindu song dedicated to the goddess Lakshmi."

Ms. Aguilar turned the music up and encouraged the class to move about the room and look at the lamps and the lights. She explained that she had a hard time choosing a song for the class because there were thousands of songs written about Diwali. All of these songs expressed the joy of coming together as a family and as a culture to celebrate this time of year.

It was all so strange to Emma — the lights, the colors, the music, and the scent of the candles. It all made her a little dizzy. She looked at her classmates. Some were laughing at the incomprehensible lyrics; some had stopped paying attention and were now whispering to one another. She couldn't stop thinking about Arjun. She wondered if Arjun found his new home as strange and difficult to understand as she did the lyrics of this song.

Chapter 5

A Strange and Lonely Place

On the way home, Emma sat alone on the bus. It wasn't really by choice — Zoe and Liz were sitting together — but Emma was glad to have some time to herself.

She couldn't get the song out of her head. What did the lyrics mean? What kinds of instruments were used to play a song like that? An unprompted thought came to her: Arjun would know.

Emma suddenly felt very small.

As soon as she got home, Emma asked her mom for permission to use the computer in order to search for information on Diwali. While she was searching, she also learned that a Hindu is someone who practices Hinduism, which in India was a major religion and an important part of Indian culture. There were so many traditions involved with Hinduism that Emma quickly got lost in all the information she found.

Emma groaned with embarrassment. She suddenly realized that Arjun probably didn't understand anything she'd said about Thanksgiving turkeys and Christmas trees. It made sense now why he didn't say anything. He must have been thinking about Diwali, a beautiful and fun celebration that nobody in his new home knew about.

Emma lay awake in bed that night. She tried to imagine what it would be like to live in a place where nobody knew about Thanksgiving or Christmas. The stores wouldn't sell turkeys or any of the holiday treats she had become so used to eating on those special days. She imagined not being able to buy a Christmas tree because nobody sold it. She then realized with horror that she would probably have to go to school during the holidays!

Emma's imagination kept spinning out horrible scenarios. She imagined living in a place where she didn't know anyone and where no one cared about the music she listened to, the shows she watched, or the holidays that mattered most to her. She tried to see her world the way Arjun saw it, and it was a strange and lonely place.

It didn't take long for Emma to make up her mind. She would apologize to Arjun. She would have to find a way to make up for the way she had behaved.

Chapter 6

A Great Day

Arjun was at school the next day. When the time came for their daily meeting, Arjun seemed oddly nervous, but he also had a look of determination on his face. Emma sat down across from Arjun and took a deep breath. She hadn't figured out what to say.

To Emma's surprise, Arjun spoke first. "I just wanted to tell you," he said softly and with an accent, "that I am sorry for the way I have been the last few days." Emma was so shocked that she couldn't say anything in response, so Arjun continued. "I was really rude. I wanted to help with the project, really, but I do not know much about Thanksgiving, and I have never decorated a Christmas tree." He sighed. "I guess I am just feeling sorry for myself, because right now, at home in India — "

"It's Diwali!" Emma jumped in. Arjun's eyes lit up at her words. "I know," Emma continued. "Ms. Aguilar had a whole class about it yesterday. I'm sorry you missed it. She played us music and had hung up lanterns and everything."

"Yes!" Arjun cried. "Diwali! It is — it is — " He seemed to be struggling to find the proper word.

"It's amazing," said Emma.

Arjun nodded with pride and said, "It really is!"

Emma and Arjun sat in silence for a moment, smiling at each other. Then Arjun shook his head and was serious again.

He said, "But even though I am missing home, I should never have been so rude. I am really sorry."

Emma laughed. She was supposed to be the one apologizing. In fact, she remembered, she still hadn't. She cleared her throat. "Um, I'm sorry too. I can't imagine how strange everything must seem to you. I was really selfish to only talk about my family's holiday traditions," she admitted.

Suddenly, Emma knew what she needed to do to make it up to Arjun.

"How about we pick a tradition from your culture? We can do a presentation on an Indian or a Hindu celebration."

Again Arjun was surprised, but then he realized what had happened. "You looked it up!"

Emma laughed and nodded.

The rest of their meeting flew by. Arjun offered suggestions for some Hindu traditions celebrated by his family, and Emma took notes on each. They agreed to choose the most fun and beautiful celebration from the list for their project. Mr. Grady watched them with an approving smile.

On the bus ride home, Emma sat by the window and rehearsed one more apology she still had to make. Maybe tomorrow, she thought, she could apologize to Zoe and Liz and invite Arjun to play with them during recess.

Emma gazed out the window and hummed a tune. She realized suddenly it was the Diwali song that Ms. Aguilar had played for the class. It really was catchy.

Emma sat back, letting the music fill her head, along with the memories of her surprisingly great day.